For the curious, questioning and brave.

Thank you to the wonderful Gina McCrudden for tidying up my writing, and to the amazing Catherine Casey for her unbeatable enthusiasm and enormous help with this project; I couldn't have a better team to work with!

Thank you to Pádraic Fogarty at the Irish Wildlife Trust, and to Michael Viney at Irish Times for their reviews added to the back cover – having this type of support made me feel I'm on the right track with this book.

Thank you Sine Queen for the remarkable title.

Thank you to Giorgio and David, the two most important people in my life, for being the first readers and critics of this book.

First published in Ireland by Natural World Publishing, 2021
www.naturalworldpublishing.ie

ISBN 978-1-5272-9320-5

© 2021 Aga Grandowicz
Edited by Gina McCrudden
Scientific consultation by Catherine Casey
Printed in Ireland by Rymar Print

To see Aga Grandowicz's other wildlife projects, follow her Instagram account at *@AgaGrandowicz*. To buy Aga's original artwork or prints, visit her website at *www.aga-grandowicz.com*. To book her for art commissions or art workshops, email her at *contact@aga-grandowicz.com*

Aga Grandowicz

REMARKABLE CREATURES:

a guide to some of Ireland's disappearing animals

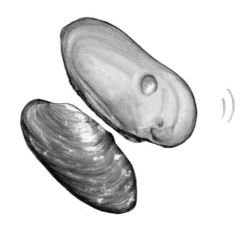

NATURAL
WORLD
PUBLISHING.

Wildlife
Adventure
Club

OUTDOOR MINI
SURVIVAL KIT

INTRODUCTION

We're lucky to share our planet with so many remarkable creatures. Just like any shared space, everything in it is connected and that's a truly wonderful thing – it means we're all part of the same ecosystem and each of us needs to protect it.

Take the humble bee, for example. Bees are one of the most important and impressive creatures we live alongside, with more than 20,000 species pollinating nearly 370,000 different plants, all over the world.

They're just one of the millions of living things that help the planet by simply doing the job they were born to do. Like the lush forests that work like giant lungs to clean our air, the endless miles of hard-working hedgerows that protect us from flooding, and less obvious little creatures like earthworms, working tirelessly underfoot, to keep our soil rich and fertile.

We're surrounded by wonders that give us everything we need to stay happy and healthy. But one creature hasn't been playing its part and I'm afraid to say, it's us.

People are the biggest risk to the planet right now, with thousands of mammals, birds and amphibians all in danger of becoming extinct if we don't do more to protect the environment and the places they call home.

Our wildlife is suffering in Ireland too, with 2,450 species at risk and over 270 plants, vertebrates and invertebrates on the brink of extinction*.

There is good news, however. We can still make a difference and you, my friend, are the best person to do it.

Join me, as I travel throughout the island of Ireland. I'll introduce you to some of our most endangered species and maybe someday soon, you can play your part to help save them.

Time is running out, so we need to act fast. Let's get started.

Aga

*According to The State of Nature report published by The National Biodiversity Network (nbn.org.uk), quoted from Irish Post, in the article by Harry Brent, October 04, 2019

FRESHWATER PEARL MUSSEL
(Margaritifera margaritifera)

HORSETAIL SLOTH WEEVIL
(Bagous lutulentus)

GREAT YELLOW BUMBLEBEE
(Bombus distinguendus)

THRIFT CLEARWING
(Pyropteron (Synansphecia) muscaeformis)

WALL BROWN
(Lasiommata megera)

ATLANTIC SALMON
(Salmo salar)

EUROPEAN EEL
(Anguilla anguilla)
PAGE 18

SPINY DOGFISH
(Squalus acanthias)
PAGE 20

WHITE SKATE
(Rostroraja alba)
PAGE 22

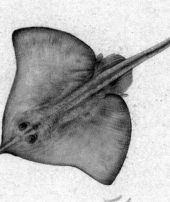

TWITE
(Carduelis flavirostris)
PAGE 24

EURASIAN CURLEW
(Numenius arquata)
PAGE 26

BARN OWL
(Tyto alba)
PAGE 28

GOLDEN EAGLE
(Aquila chrysaetos)
PAGE 30

FRESHWATER PEARL MUSSEL (Margaritifera margaritifera)

Freshwater pearl mussels are amazing for lots of reasons but let's start with the fact that they can live for over 130 years. Valeriy Zyuganov, a famous malacologist (that's someone who studies molluscs like mussels, slugs, snails and squid), estimated that freshwater pearl mussels could reach the grand old age of 250.

We know of one specimen found in Estonia that celebrated its 134th birthday. The researcher doesn't say what happened to the mussel after it was caught, but I like to think it was set free to enjoy an even longer life.

> ### Did you know?
> You can tell a mussel's age by counting the dark lines or ridges on its shell. They represent winter rest periods – just like the rings on a tree trunk can be counted to accurately work out the tree's age.

Despite this wonderful little mollusc's ability to live so long, freshwater pearl mussels are a critically endangered species, and not only in Ireland. As filter feeders, they get everything they need from food particles found in the 50 litres of water they inhale and expel each day. To do this, juvenile mussels need clean, well-oxygenated riverbeds, which are sadly in decline.

As a species, they're vulnerable to even slight changes in their environment. Things like drainage, sewage disposal and water pollution caused by humans play a big part in their ever-decreasing numbers.

Freshwater pearl mussels also have complex reproduction cycles involving salmonid fish like salmon, so anything that affects their survival has a knock-on effect for our freshwater friend.

Populations of European freshwater pearl mussels have dropped by a devastating 90% in the last 100 years. Today, 27 populations are protected in Special Areas of Conservation in the Republic of Ireland, and only three substantial populations exist in Northern Ireland – in the Claddagh (Swanlinbar) River, the Owenkillew River and the Upper Ballinderry River.

FAST FACTS

Size: 12-15 cm.

Habitat: Clean, fast-flowing streams and rivers with fine gravel and coarse sand, between 50 cm and 2 m deep.
The presence of salmonids like salmon or trout in the same water is essential, as freshwater pearl mussels rely on them for the first nine months of their life, when they live attached to these fish gills (without causing any harm to the fish).

Conservation status in Ireland: Critically endangered.

Reasons for being endangered: Reduction in water quality and changes to habitat caused by human activity.

Learn more about freshwater pearl mussels in Ireland at _pearlmusselproject.ie_

(ACTIVITY)

Make a water filter.

You can clean dirty water with a few things you'll find around your home.

Take a large, empty plastic bottle and cut out the bottom part. You can ask an adult if you need help with this bit. Cover the bottleneck with a piece of cloth (muslin works great) and secure it with some string.

Turn the bottle upside down and fill it with fine sand, cold charcoal, small bits of gravel, little twigs and pebbles. Pop the bottle in a bucket or basin and, through the side you cut open, pour dirty water with things like soil and crushed leaves in it.

The water that flows out the other side should be much cleaner than the water you're pouring in. A simple but perfect example of how large water filters work in running rivers, on a much smaller scale.

dirty water

twigs and pebbles

small gravel

charcoal

sand

piece of cloth

cleaner water

7

HORSETAIL SLOTH WEEVIL (Bagous lutulentus)

This semi-aquatic beetle provides us with a challenging scavenger hunt – it's so rare you can find it only in a handful of Irish coastal locations. However, the clue to finding it is in the name because horsetail sloth weevil only feeds on one plant – water horsetail (*Equisetum fluviatile*).

Unlike its water-loving relatives, this weevil spends quite a lot of time above the water, so it's worth extending your search to look in fens (a type of a wetland) and shallow water where water horsetail grows. Warm, dry days in June and July are best for spotting these tiny beetles, and your chances increase if you're in counties Wexford, Waterford, Galway or Kerry in the Republic of Ireland and counties Fermanagh, Tyrone, Antrim or Down in Northern Ireland.

TIP
Horsetail sloth weevils measure only up to 3.3 mm, so have a magnifying glass to support your search.

Weevils are insects and members of the order Coleoptera, also known as the beetles. All weevils have a distinctive long snout, and that's part of the reason for their success, as they use it not only for feeding but also for boring holes to lay their eggs. Unfortunately, this means that some weevils cause damage to crops and are considered pests. Luckily, horsetail sloth weevil's favourite plant is not cultivated for human consumption; therefore, this little beetle is rather unlikely to bother anyone.

Did you know?
We've discovered over sixty thousand weevil species, making them the single largest group of living organisms on Earth!

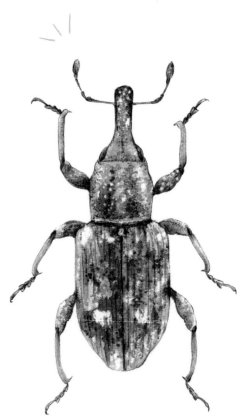

water horsetail

FAST FACTS

Size: 2.2-3.3 mm.

Habitat: Wetlands covered in water horsetail.

Conservation status in Ireland: Critically endangered.

Reasons for being endangered: Habitat drainage and pollution.

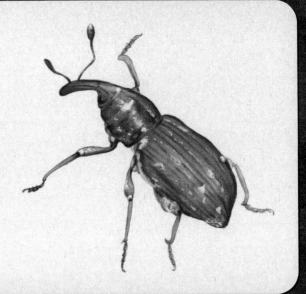

ACTIVITY

Check the water quality in your nearby river by discovering which insects live there.

Some insects will only live in particularly clean water, others can tolerate a bit of pollution. Use the card shown here to see if you can spot any of these creatures in your river.

To learn more about Irish aquatic life and to engage in conservation of our waters, visit _streamscapes.ie_

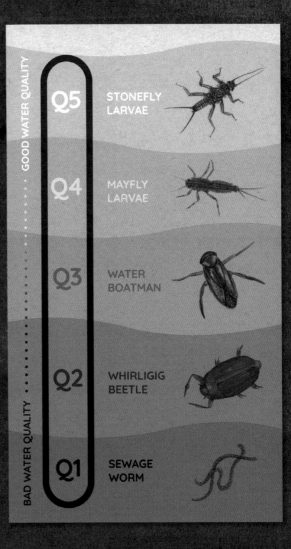

GOOD WATER QUALITY

Q5 — STONEFLY LARVAE

Q4 — MAYFLY LARVAE

Q3 — WATER BOATMAN

Q2 — WHIRLIGIG BEETLE

Q1 — SEWAGE WORM

BAD WATER QUALITY

GREAT YELLOW BUMBLEBEE *(Bombus distinguendus)*

Great yellow bumblebee queens take comfort in a prolonged winter sleep and emerge from hibernation much later than the other bumblebee species in Ireland. They hold off until mid-May or June when it's warmer, and the risk of frost is long gone.

It's no coincidence; it also happens to be the time of year when its favourite flowering plant, the red clover (which is pink!), is in full bloom. Great yellow bumblebee has never been common across Ireland but was widespread – in small numbers. These days however, with the number of rich red clover meadows falling, so too is the great yellow bumblebee.

The fact that they hibernate for so long doesn't help their cause because it shortens the time available to complete the bumblebee's life cycle. So, if the flowers they need are limited or, worse, not present at all, the great yellow bumblebee won't be able to produce enough offspring each season to keep the population growing.

Great yellow bumblebees typically nest underground in tussocky grasslands and dunes with flowering plants.

> **Tussocky grasses** usually grow as singular plants in clumps, or bunches, rather than forming a lawn that you might see in your park or garden.

You'll find lots of places like this along the west coast of Ireland – perfect for bumbling buddies and their queen. She's bigger than the others at around 2 cm long, making her one of the largest bumblebees in Ireland.

The healthiest populations of great yellow bumblebees are now found on the Mullet Peninsula in County Mayo in the Republic of Ireland and close to Newcastle in Northern Ireland.

FAST FACTS

Size: Queens can reach up to 2 cm in length.

Habitat: Tussocky grasses and flowering grasslands with lots of red clover and common knapweed.

Conservation status in Ireland: Endangered.

Reasons for being endangered: Loss of flower-rich habitat due to changes in farming methods.

Visit _pollinators.ie_ for plenty of bees-related resources and tips.

 ACTIVITY

Make a plant tower with a rock garden.

Exposed soil and sand offer great yellow bumblebees shelter, and the flowering plants provide food.

You'll need wire mesh (chicken wire), some pieces of bendy wire, gravel, sand, soil, and a pile of medium size stones.

Choose a sunny spot in your garden. Take a piece of wire mesh (2 m long and 20 cm high is ideal), make a circle and join the ends with the bendy wire. Fill it with a mix of sand, soil, and gravel.

Repeat these steps two more times with shorter pieces of wire mesh to create a tower-like structure.

Once the tower is filled and steady, you can start sowing plants like red clover in the top part of the tower and add succulents like _Sempervivum_, ice plant, or pink _Delosperma_ to the tower's walls, filling the holes of the wire mesh.

You can decorate the bottom of the tower with larger stones and rocks and add bamboo sticks in the gaps to create homes and hiding places for bugs and solitary bees. You could even add a pole with a bee house attached to it, as your next project.

chicken wire

ready plant tower

THRIFT CLEARWING (Pyropteron (Synansphecia) muscaeformis)

If you've ever wondered what a flying lobster might look like, a thrift clearwing is probably as close as you'll get.

This dapper little creature looks like it's dressed for a special occasion with black or bronze colouring that gives way to tiny transparent gaps on its forewings, so it looks like it's wearing lace. How elegant!

This small moth finds the pink, rounded flowerheads of thrift simply irresistible. It's the same colourful thrift plant that gives the thrift clearwing its name because as caterpillars, they feast on its roots and crowns. You can easily spot thrift dotting Ireland's rocky coastlines.

What would your name be if you were named after the food that you love most?
A pasta human, burger human, fruit human? It's a pretty simple way to name a species, but it's also a great way to spot a thrift clearwing as the two (the moth and the plant) are frequently found together.

Summer is an important time for this flower-loving moth. Caterpillars are fully grown by June, and their magical transformation into a moth is complete by July.

The thrift clearwing is just one of around 1,000 known clearwing moth species. Only five are present in Ireland, one is thought to be extinct and two are currently critically endangered.

Before 1970, this little moth was a frequent visitor in Country Antrim and along the rocky coast from Howth to Clare, including Dublin, Wexford, Saltee Islands and Seven Heads. However, the numbers have fallen sharply since then, and since 2000, they have only been found in two sites in West Cork.

We don't know the exact reason for the drop in population, as the thrift clearwing's natural habitat has been well preserved and their favourite food is still in good supply – but pollution, an increased number of predators, or a disease that we're not yet aware of, could be the cause.

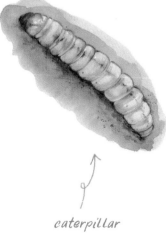

caterpillar

FAST FACTS

Size: Wingspan 12–18 mm, forewing 6-8 mm.

Habitat: Rocky coastlines where the thrift plant is present.

Conservation status in Ireland: Critically endangered.

Reasons for being endangered: Unknown.

Visit _butterflyconservation.ie_ and _butterfly-conservation.org_ to get involved in conservation of Irish butterflies, moths and their habitats.

ACTIVITY

Create a moth lampshade.

You'll need a clear, cylinder-shaped glass vase, one A4 piece of white paper and one A4 piece of dark paper, scissors, a paper knife, and a cutting mat. If you're 11 years old or younger, you should ask an adult to help.

Start by wrapping one piece of paper around the vase and measure how much it takes to go all the way around. Make a little mark and cut the two pieces of paper to that size, recycling whatever is left.

Draw two thrift clearwing moths and two or three thrift flowers on your dark paper. It's a good idea to make the shapes big and easy to cut around with your paper knife.

Wrap the vase with the white paper, then do the same with the dark paper. Use a staple to secure them in place. Finally, take an LED tealight, turn it on, pop it inside the vase and enjoy the soft glow of your beautiful new lamp.

WALL BROWN *(Lasiommata megera)*

This medium-sized butterfly with heavily patterned orange and brown wings, stays close to the coastal areas of the Republic of Ireland and Northern Ireland, taking shelter and feeding in places like disused quarries, derelict land, dry grasslands, dunes and other coastal habitats.

As caterpillars, grasses top their list of favourite food plants – with tor-grass (*Brachypodium pinnatum*), false brome (*Brachypodium sylvaticum*), cock's-foot (*Dactylis glomerata*), bents (*Agrostis capillaris*), wavy hair-grass (*Deschampsia flexuosa*) and Yorkshire-fog (*Holcus lanatus*) among the tastiest (and funniest sounding).

Adult walls emerge from May to mid-June and again from July to September.

Like so many of Ireland's native insects, this beautiful butterfly was named because of its love for basking in the sunshine on walls, rocks and bare ground, where the colour of its wings provides the perfect camouflage against stony or sandy surfaces.

Even though wall brown butterflies can produce two or even three broods (or little walls) each year, their numbers in Ireland have declined dramatically in the last 20 years, making it one of the critically endangered Irish butterfly species.

The reason for its decline inland is thought to be the loss of flowering grasslands.

> TIP
> Wall browns don't gather in large numbers and they're very alert, so binoculars or a camera with a good zoom is a must if you're on a mission to see them up close.

FAST FACTS

Size: Wingspan 45-53 mm
(male tends to be shorter, female longer).

Habitat: Usually in open, dry grasslands,
derelict land, dunes, and other coastal areas.

Conservation status in Ireland:
Critically endangered.

Reasons for being endangered:
Loss of unimproved flowering grasslands.

Visit _butterflyconservation.ie_ and _butterfly-conservation.org_ to get involved in conservation of Irish butterflies, moths and their habitats.

ACTIVITY

Make a seed butterfly.

You'll need a wooden clothes peg, markers or paints, two toothpicks, or short pieces of wire.

Decorate your peg with markers or paints, so it looks like a butterfly's body. Add eyes, a mouth and two antennae made of toothpicks or wire.

Use glue, tape or blu tack to attach them to the peg.

Close the peg down the centre of a pack of native to Ireland meadow flower seeds and give it to a nature-lover as a present.

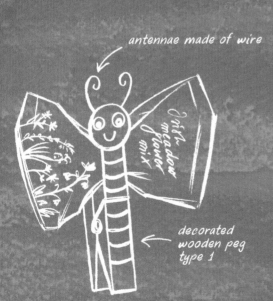

antennae made of wire

decorated wooden peg type 1

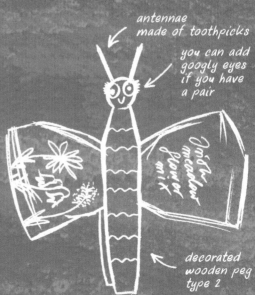

antennae made of toothpicks

you can add googly eyes if you have a pair

decorated wooden peg type 2

ATLANTIC SALMON (Salmo salar)

This large fish can grow up to 1 m long and is known as one of nature's true explorers. To broaden their horizons and taste new waters, Atlantic salmon make epic journeys, travelling from the rivers they're born in, to the depths of the Atlantic Ocean. Here, they swim, feed, and build their strength in the tough, salty water and, after a few years, travel back to the exact place where they were born.

This incredible behaviour is called natal philopatry and it's something we see in other animals, like sea turtles and bluefin tuna.

> Philopatry is the tendency of an animal to stay in or regularly return to a particular area.
>
> Natal philopatry happens when animals return to their birthplace to reproduce.

Scientists believe that a unique magnetic field exists at a salmon's place of birth and olfactory (smell-related) cues help them make their way home. It's a little like having built-in satellite navigation, which usually works very well. Some salmon take a wrong turn now and then and end up in the wrong river, but if they manage to breed in these new sites, they will have widened their breeding base and can increase the species' chances of survival.

Which begs the question...
If it's possible to breed elsewhere, why do salmon go to such great lengths to return to the river where they were born? It's simply because they trust their parents. They picked the river the salmon now calls home and it proved safe and suitable for them to survive and thrive. The way this fish sees it is – why mess with something when you know it works?

It's a perfect plan, but the river the young fish started in can change during the time they spent in the ocean. The adult salmon might return to waters that are polluted and have parasites. The river's morphology (how the river is shaped, runs and looks) might also have changed because of human activity, so even if they make the daunting journey home, breeding safely could be an even greater challenge.

female

male

FAST FACTS

Size: Up to 1 m in length.

Habitat: Cool and clean rivers (from birth to nine months) and food-rich areas of the Atlantic Ocean (above nine months).

Conservation status in Ireland: Endangered.

Reasons for being endangered: Habitat destruction, pollution, and overfishing.

Did you know?
Out of an average of 4,000 eggs laid, only two fish will survive in the ocean and make it home to breed!

ACTIVITY

Osmosis.

Moving between freshwater and saltwater changes the balance of water and salt in a salmon's body. This balance is called an osmotic balance and it's controlled by osmoregulation.

Without osmoregulation, salmon would have a very high salt concentration in their body while at sea – leading to dehydration, and in freshwater, they'd suffer from salt loss and water loading.

The regulation of osmosis – passing of fluid through salmon's semi-permeable membranes (including skin) from an area of high concentration to one of lower concentration – is therefore essential for salmon's survival.

Imitate osmosis with a potato.

Take two small bowls and fill them with an inch of water. Add two tablespoons of salt to one of the bowls and and pop a label on or next to it.

Slice one potato lengthwise and make some chip-shaped pieces.

Place an equal number of pieces in each bowl (two or three is plenty) and leave them to rest in the water for 20 minutes.

The potatoes in the salty water will become mushy through osmosis. This happens because the higher concentration of salt in the water surrounding the potatoes pushes the water out of the potato pieces and into the surrounding water, in an attempt to balance the salt levels.

The potato pieces in the salt-free water will remain unchanged.

To learn more about salmon's conservation efforts in Ireland, visit salmonwatchireland.ie

EUROPEAN EEL *(Anguilla anguilla)*

Just like Atlantic salmon, European eels don't hang around too long in their place of birth. For them, life begins in the salty waters of the Sargasso Sea in the Atlantic Ocean and they migrate as larvae (known as glass eels because they are transparent and their skin is almost colourless) to freshwater rivers far from where they were born.

Long life is something the European eel enjoys too, with captive specimens living over 80 years. A rather famous one called the Brantevik Eel lived for 155 years in the well of a Swedish family in Brantevik!

European eels spend anything from five to 20 years in freshwater before travelling back to the Sargasso Sea to breed. For eels living in Irish rivers, that means a journey of more than 4,000 km which can take up to 100 days.

They're one of only fifteen native fish found in Ireland's freshwater habitats and the population in the Republic of Ireland has suffered a considerable decline. Since the 1980s, the number of glass eels (remember that's eel larvae) in our rivers has dropped to less than 7% of what it was previously.

This is considered a serious environmental issue and living proof that the health of our oceans, estuaries, and freshwaters has deteriorated significantly over the last forty years.

The survival of European eels is helped by the fact that their blood is poisonous, so many would-be predators are discouraged from eating them. Even a tiny amount of eel blood is enough to kill a person, so only a well-cooked eel should ever be eaten.

FAST FACTS

Size: 60-150 cm in length.

Habitat: Sargasso Sea in the Atlantic Ocean from birth to its larvae stage, then freshwater rivers.

Conservation status in Ireland: Critically endangered.

Reasons for being endangered: Habitat loss due to human activity, pollutants, predation, disease, parasites, overfishing, and barriers preventing migration, like weirs and hydroelectric dams. Possibly also changes in ocean currents and/or temperature – likely due to climate change.

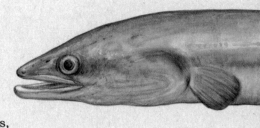

Did you know?
Even though their population is so endangered, eels are still commercially fished in Ireland!

ACTIVITY

Check your local river for eels.

Glass eels
Young eels are transparent and almost colourless, which means you can see all their internal organs.

Yellow eels
Grown-up eels take their name after the brownish-yellow colour that runs along their sides and belly.

Elvers
Miniature adult eels.

Silver eels
Mature eels are at least five years old and ready to travel back to the Sargasso Sea to breed.

SPINY DOGFISH (Squalus acanthias)

What an odd name for a fish, you're thinking, and you're right. It doesn't have fur, it doesn't bark, and it definitely won't fetch a stick, so why the name?

The spiny dogfish has a few names including spurdog, piked dogfish, spiky dog, white spotted dogfish and even rock salmon (if you don't happen to be a dog person).

The story goes that a fisherman came up with this name after watching these sharks chase smaller fish in large, dog-like packs.

And yes, the spiny dogfish is a shark. At only 70 to 100 cm long, it's much smaller than the basking sharks that visit Irish waters and completely harmless to humans, although their spines do contain a toxin that can cause painful wounds.

Unfortunately, it's not the same the other way around. Humans love spiny dogfish meat and the population has dropped so rapidly because of overfishing that this harmless little shark is now an endangered species in the Republic of Ireland. The numbers have dropped so low that fishing the species is no longer allowed in the European Union. Unfortunately, they can still be caught by accident. This is known as 'by-catch'.

The reputation of spiny dogfish for chewing through fishermen's nets to eat their catch hasn't helped them make friends, but the numbers in North-East Atlantic are better, so maybe spiny dogfish and fishermen on that side of Ireland are on better terms.

It's believed spiny dogfish can live up to 70 years. How do we know that? Just like with trees and the freshwater pearl mussel, marine biologists count growth rings - for sharks, these are on the vertebrae.

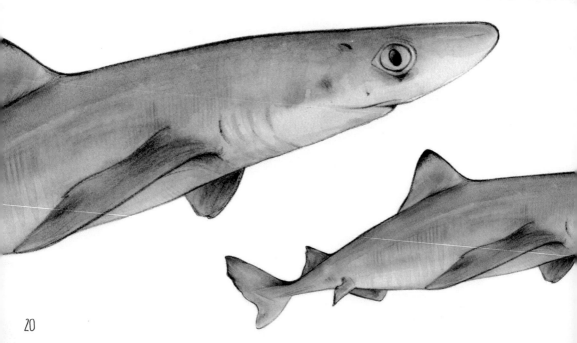

FAST FACTS

Size: Up to 1 m in length, males are smaller than females.

Habitat: Temperate continental shelf seas, usually in waters less than 200 m deep.

Conservation status in Ireland: Endangered in the Republic of Ireland.

Reasons for being endangered: Habitat damage due to heavy fishing equipment, overfishing (particularly pregnant females), late sexual maturity, and slow reproduction rates which limit population recovery after exploitation.

Visit the Irish Elasmobranch Group to learn more about conservation of sharks, skates, rays and chimaeras in Irish waters; irishelasmobranchgroup.com

 ACTIVITY

Make your own faux shark tooth fossil.

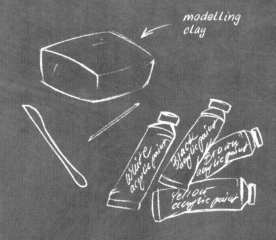

modelling clay

Sharks continually shed and replace their teeth, with some species working their way through 35,000 teeth in their lifetime (the shark tooth fairy must be especially busy!). That's why it's not uncommon to find a shark tooth, even a fossilised one on a beach or in the ocean.

Until you find your own, we can create a replica with modelling clay.

You'll need white clay (the kind that goes hard when baked), a few sculpting tools (a mini spatula or toothpick will work), and acrylic paints in yellow, brown, white, and black.

ready tooth

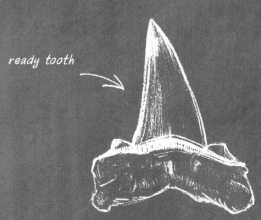

Shape the tooth using your hands. The sculpting tools will help to create little creases. Bake the tooth according to the instructions on the modelling clay packaging. When it's cold, you can get to work with your paints.

WHITE SKATE (Rostroraja alba)

Gliding along the sandy ocean bed like a flying carpet, this cartilaginous fish moves with skill and speed. It's an expert diver too, so it can disappear quickly from the water's surface to a depth of up to 400 m.

> Sharks and rays are other examples of cartilaginous fish, meaning they have cartilage instead of bones – a resilient and smooth elastic tissue, just like we have in our ears.

Unfortunately for the white skate, it's a rather tasty fish too, so it can end up on someone's dinner plate just as fast!

If you research this fish (also known as bottlenose or spearnose skate), most of the information you'll find is about how to prepare and cook it, so it's hardly surprising they are now critically endangered in Ireland and across Europe. In recent years, the only records of white skate we have are from Tralee and Galway Bay in the Republic of Ireland and County Derry in Northern Ireland.

If uninterrupted, white skate can live a long life and reach up to two metres in length. Slow growth and the fact that they produce so few offspring mean not enough baby skates make it to adulthood and their dwindling population is dangerously overfished.

Skates move and look like rays – great, mesmerising flatfish that appear to fly through the water – but the main difference is that skates lay eggs in little capsules known as a mermaid's purse, while rays give birth to live young.

It's not unusual to find a precious mermaid's purse washed up on beaches, and local shark and ray sighting groups record findings to help keep track of the species. If you find any, you can add yours to the records at marinedimensions.ie

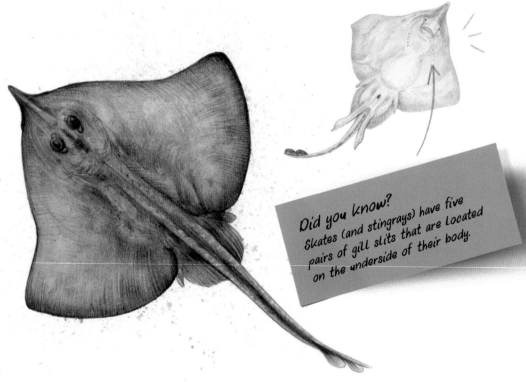

> Did you know?
> Skates (and stingrays) have five pairs of gill slits that are located on the underside of their body.

FAST FACTS

Size: Up to 2 m in length.

Habitat: Rocky, sandy, and detrital bottoms at depths of 40–400 m in the Atlantic, Mediterranean, and the Southwest Indian Ocean.

Conservation status in Ireland: Critically endangered.

Reasons for being endangered: Overfishing.

Visit the Irish Elasmobranch Group to learn more about conservation of sharks, skates, rays and chimaeras in Irish waters: irishelasmobranchgroup.com

 **ACTIVITY**

Mermaid's purse spotting.

Any excuse to walk and explore the beach is a good one. Beautiful shells and strange aquatic plants are just some of the finds that will keep you entertained, but this activity is all about the magical mermaid's purse.

Not every explorer finds one, so if luck is on your side and you manage to spot one on your local beach, be sure to take a photo or draw it, pop it back in the sea and add your sighting to the other purses listed on marinedimensions.ie

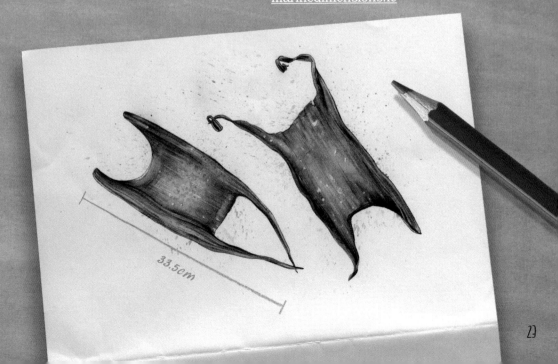

33.5cm

TWITE (Carduelis flavirostris)

Enveloped in modest brown feathers, this small finch hides among tall grasses and flowering weeds. Twites nest in heather, but they find all the nutrients they need in seeds and the buds of wild plants that grow along the Irish coast and in arable (crop-growing) fields filled with dandelion, sorrel, annual meadow grass and thistle.

Changing agricultural practices have however seen this type of vegetation being lost on a large scale, seriously reducing the breeding habitat and threatening this little bird's survival.

Based on the last survey (carried out in 1999), it was believed we had as few as 100 breeding pairs left in the Republic of Ireland and even less in Northern Ireland, with only 10 pairs recorded.

To increase your chances of spotting this well-camouflaged bird, it's worth visiting coastal bogs near weedy grasslands in counties Mayo and Donegal in April and May, which is their breeding season. Or later in the year along the north, northwest and northeast coasts where wintering populations increase as Irish birds are joined by some Scottish ones, and are easier to find.

Did you know?
Just like us, twite likes to update its summer and winter looks – it sports a bright yellow bill in winter and a soft grey one in summer.

FAST FACTS

Size: 13 to 13.5 cm in length with a wingspan of 23 cm.

Habitat: Heather, grasslands and arable fields.

Conservation status in Ireland: Critically endangered – Birds of Conservation Concern Red List.

Reasons for being endangered: Habitat loss caused by intensive farming and overgrazing of heather hillsides.

Visit _birdwatchireland.ie_ to learn more about Irish wild birds, and to get involved in protecting them.

Try frottage art.

To help us draw well-camouflaged animals, we can use a technique called frottage.

To get started, all you need is a piece of paper and a pencil. Find a rough surface, like the bark of a tree in your garden, a rough patch on the ground, or even a leaf. Press the paper against it and rub it with the pencil.

Once you've created a nice textured background, draw the bird's shape over the top of it, adding some shading and colour, and – hey presto – you have your very own little twite.

EURASIAN CURLEW (Numenius arquata)

It's enough to look at the Eurasian curlew's long, slightly bent beak and long legs to guess where it's most at home. A typical wetlands bird, it probes deep into wet mud in search of worms, insect larva, molluscs (snails and slugs), and crustaceans (prawns).

But how does it find food in mud so thick you can't see through it?
Inside the tip of this clever bird's bill (or beak), the curlew has sensory receptors that can detect food by assessing the difference in pressure between live organisms and rocks, for example.

Despite its fantastic ability to find food, it's believed the breeding population of curlew in the Republic of Ireland has dropped by as much as 97% over the last 40 years. Making this now very rare bird another critically endangered species on our island. The number of breeding pairs is estimated at less than 150 pairs in the Republic of Ireland, while Northern Ireland is believed to have between 200 and 500 pairs.

Loss of habitat is the main cause for such a drastic decline, with much of the damp unimproved/semi-improved herb-rich pastures, rushy grasslands, and boglands that curlew loves so much, under constant threat. With curlew numbers now so low and their habitat so fragmented, predation has become an important factor in their continuing decline.

Modern farming methods, drainage of wetlands, loss of boglands, and afforestation (planting trees and forests where there was no previous tree cover) have all lead to habitat loss for curlew. At the same time, the rising numbers of predators like foxes, crows, and pine martens put the curlew's eggs and young chicks in greater danger.

If you spot a curlew between April and June, please report it to the National Parks and Wildlife Service at Agri.Ecology@chg.gov.ie

TIP
Eurasian curlew likes to hang out in rushes - grass-like plants with long, hard cylinder-shaped stalks or hollows that offer shelter, shade and food.

FAST FACTS

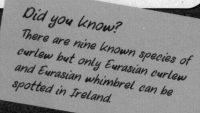

Size: 50–60 cm in length, with a wingspan of 89–106 cm.

Habitat: Wetlands and coastal environments in winter. Wet grasslands, rushy pastures, upland and lowland bogs in the breeding season.

Conservation status in Ireland: Critically endangered – Birds of Conservation Concern Red List.

Reasons for being endangered: Habitat loss caused by modern farming methods, predation, loss of bogs, and afforestation.

Did you know?
There are nine known species of curlew but only Eurasian curlew and Eurasian whimbrel can be spotted in Ireland.

Match birds with their beaks.

The shape of a bird's beak is closely linked to its favourite food and feeding habits. Check out the chart below and see how many birds you can match up with these perfectly designed beaks.

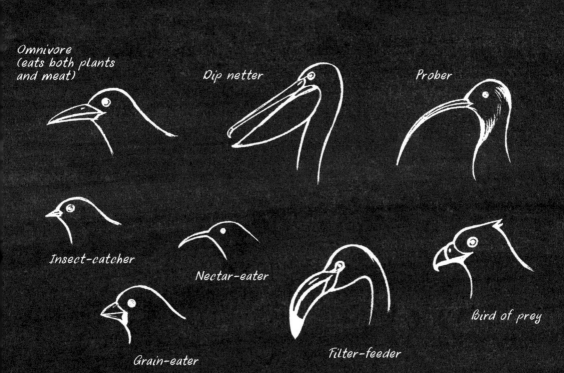

Omnivore (eats both plants and meat)

Dip netter

Prober

Insect-catcher

Nectar-eater

Grain-eater

Filter-feeder

Bird of prey

BARN OWL *(Tyto alba)*

With its sophisticated taste for nesting places, barn owls look for places like ruined castles, abandoned buildings and nice lofty barns to settle down in. Somewhere quiet and cosy with a convenient source of food, like small rodents, is perfect.

> **Did you know?**
> A pair of barn owls can eat as many as 3,000 rodents a year! Farmers love them but the farmers' cats aren't huge fans of the competition.

Indeed, it seems that the barn owl's survival is linked closely to the availability of its prey of small mammals like field mice, house mice, greater white-tooted shrew, bank voles, and brown rats. Small birds and frogs are on the menu too.

Intensification of agriculture, especially reduction in prey-rich habitat to forage in, using rodenticides to control rodents and increases in road collisions, have all contributed to the decline in barn owls.

Sadly, this beautiful bird of prey is now the most threatened owl species in the Republic of Ireland. It's estimated that there are less than 500 nesting pairs in the whole of Ireland, most of which are in the Southwest.

To see this magnificent creature is a rare and wonderful treat. Barn owls like to put their feet up during the day, but you can increase your chances of spotting them by visiting woodland edge or farmland at dusk or during the night, when they hunt for food.

> **Did you know?**
> Barn owls don't hoot – they shriek. And because their soft feathers aren't waterproof, they avoid the rain, wherever possible.

FAST FACTS

Size: 37-39 cm tall with a wingspan of around 85 cm.

Habitat: Rough grasslands, woodland edges, farmlands, and wetlands.

Conservation status in Ireland: Critically endangered – Birds of Conservation Concern Red List.

Reasons for being endangered: Loss of nesting sites, rodenticide poisoning, declining numbers of their small mammal prey of greater white-tooted shrew, and road kills.

Barn owls are monitored by Barn Owl Project, BirdTrack and Countryside Bird Survey. Check them out to learn more.

ACTIVITY

Build an owl nesting box.

With fewer nesting sites available for barn owls, we can help them by building special nesting boxes.

Ask an adult to help you with this task and use the blueprint below.

Once built, the nesting box can be fixed to an exposed tree trunk, or the inside or outside of a shed where passing owls may find it.

It's best to locate it where there is good habitat for food and little risk of rodenticide use.

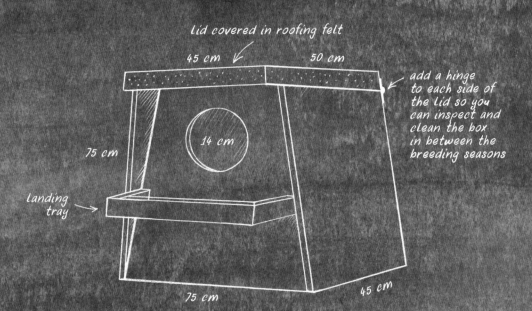

lid covered in roofing felt

45 cm   50 cm

add a hinge to each side of the lid so you can inspect and clean the box in between the breeding seasons

14 cm

75 cm

landing tray

75 cm   45 cm

GOLDEN EAGLE *(Aquila chrysaetos)*

An important feature in mythology, a national symbol for several countries, and the centre of countless logos and brand images, the golden eagle has always represented power, courage, and strength. A majestic and highly respected animal, it is undoubtedly the king of the skies.

> **Did you know?**
> Native Americans attach special significance to eagles, with images of the birds and their feathers used down the ages and real feathers presented to honour the most respected within tribes and indigenous cultures.

Golden eagles fly higher and see better than any other bird in the Irish sky, and they're strong enough to fly long distances. These master divers can attack their prey (hares, rabbits, foxes, and birds) at up to 320 km per hour, which is about the speed of a racing Ferrari!

After being hunted to extinction in Ireland in the early 1900s, golden eagles were reintroduced in 2001. We now have a small population hovering in a few areas of County Donegal, and – if their habitat is managed to improve the availability of their food prey – it's hoped they will breed for many years to come.

Golden eagles hunt in open or semi-open mountainous areas, are active all year round and stick to daylight hours for the most part. They avoid urban, agricultural, and heavily forested regions, so get ready to spend some time in the great outdoors, if you want to see one soar.

> **Did you know?**
> Golden eagles can live up to 30 years.

FAST FACTS

Size: 66 to 102 cm long, with a wingspan of 1.8 to 2.34 m.

Habitat: Food-rich open or semi-open mountainous areas.

Conservation status in Ireland: Critically endangered. Red-listed, after being extinct and then slowly reintroduced.

Reasons for being endangered: Human activity like hunting, persecution, accidental poisoning (intended for other species), collisions with man-made objects, and lack of food.

Visit _goldeneagle.ie_ to learn more about the golden eagle's conservation in Ireland.

Design a logo featuring a golden eagle.

Create a golden eagle logo that could be used by a nature trust or sports club. Remember all the great things the eagle symbolises and work them into your design.

You can even ask your teacher to suggest this as an art project at school.

Notes on conservation

by Catherine Casey, Heritage Officer at Laois County Council

To target conservation work to where it's needed most, researchers use an international standard to decide how threatened – or how close to extinction – a species is. This standard is set by the International Union for the Conservation of Nature (IUCN). The IUCN assess species at a global level and divides species into nine categories:

- Not evaluated
- Data deficient
- Least concern
- Near threatened
- Vulnerable, endangered
- Critically endangered
- Extinct in the wild
- Extinct

Species that are threatened with extinction are put on the IUCN Red List.

In Ireland, we use the same categories to describe how certain species are doing in this country and Red Lists have been published for plants, bees, beetles, freshwater fish, sharks, rays, and more. For birds, the fourth Red List of Bird of Conservation Concern was published in 2021 by **BirdWatch Ireland** (the first one was in 1998).

Today, 37,400 species are threatened with extinction globally. Sadly, this is 28% of all species assessed. The species in this book are all listed as endangered or critically endangered in Ireland.

A look at the reasons why species are threatened shows up some common concerns. In most cases, there are issues with their habitat or the places they live. Whether that is the management of farmland, woodland, or the quality of the water they live in, we need to start making improvements in their habitats to ensure the species will survive. Other common factors include activities by humans, like building roads, use of pesticides, and overfishing.

What can we do?
You've made the first step by being interested and finding out more about some of our most endengered species.

- We can do many things in our own gardens to help pollinators – visit **pollinators.ie** for gardening tips.
- We can all plant more trees and feed birds in winter.
- We can try to eat local food, when it's in season.
- We can talk to those around us about our concern for the natural world.
- We can connect with like-minded people and support valuable conservation by joining conservation groups like **BirdWatch Ireland, the Irish Wildlife Trust** and **an Taisce**.
- And most of all, we can stay curious, keep learning and find out all we can about our natural world and how it works.

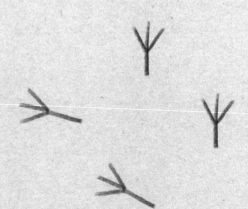

Some of the animals extinct in Ireland

- Grey whale *(Eschrichtius robustus)*
- Irish elk *(Megaloceros giganteus)*
- Brown bear *(Ursus arctos)*
- Grey wolf *(Canis lupus)*
- Eurasian lynx *(Lynx lynx)*
- Wildcat *(Felis silvestris)*
- Great auk *(Pinguinus impennis)*
- Corn bunting *(Emberiza calandra)*
- Mountain ringlet *(Erebia epiphron)*
- Hornet clearwing moth *(Sesia apiformis)*
- Solitary bee *(Nomada sheppardana)*
- Mud pond snail *(Omphiscola glabra)*

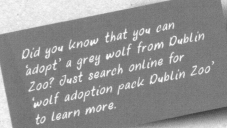

Did you know that you can 'adopt' a grey wolf from Dublin Zoo? Just search online for 'wolf adoption pack Dublin Zoo' to learn more.

SAVE IRELAND'S REMARKABLE CREATURES

Thanks for reading and getting involved.

You can be a great friend to Ireland's most remarkable creatures and any friend of nature is a friend of mine!

Take care of yourself and your surroundings.

Love,
Aga Grandowicz

Your notes and sightings